MW00529743

# GOD HIDDEN,
# WHEREABOUTS UNKNOWN

# GOD HIDDEN,
# *WHEREABOUTS UNKNOWN*

The Holy Ari and the 'Contraction' of God

*Third Expanded Edition*

NETANEL MILES-YÉPEZ
*&* ZALMAN SCHACHTER-SHALOMI

## Albion
### *Andalus*

Boulder, Colorado
*2021*

*"The old shall be renewed,
and the new shall be made holy."*

— Rabbi Avraham Yitzhak Kook

Albion-Andalus Inc.
P. O. Box 19852
Boulder, CO 80308
www.albionandalus.com

Design and composition by Albion-Andalus Inc.
Cover design by D.A.M. Cool Graphics
Cover art of "Ari HaKodesh" by Netanel Miles-Yépez

ISBN: 978-1-953220-00-4 (HC)
ISBN: 978-1-953220-01-1 (PB)

Manufactured in the United States of America

*"The* tzimtzum *was a result of God's love."*

— The Maggid of Mezritch

# CONTENTS

# PREFACE TO THE THIRD EDITION

THIS LITTLE BOOK WAS originally inspired by a talk that Rabbi Zalman Schachter-Shalomi, *z"l*, gave to B'nai Or Religious Fellowship students on January 8th, 1985, called "Tzimtzum."

In 1999, Reb Zalman, as he is more generally known, gave me the transcript of this talk in response to a request for sources on *tzimtzum,* as I was then writing my master's thesis on the concepts of *ayin* in kabbalistic Judaism and *shunyata* in Vajrayana Buddhism. Taken by the raw brilliance of its ideas, I immediately began to develop the talk into a longer work, exploring paradigm shift and the more philosophical aspects of *tzimtzum.* It was my first writing collaboration with him.

Part I of this book (offering a short biography of Rabbi Yitzhak Luria, as well as a small collection of stories told of him) has been added to this third edition to give readers a short introduction to the Ari before launching into a wide-ranging exploration of his concept of *tzimtzum.* These stories were originally collected and retold for an unrealized project of my own re-examining the Ari's more profound ideas. The story, "Hallahs in the Ark," however, was originally re-told by Reb Zalman for *The Holy Beggar's Gazette.*

Part II is largely my own exploration of the evolution of the idea of *tzimtzum* through different historical paradigms based upon teachings from Reb Zalman in his original "Tzimtzum" talk, integrating much of that material.

Part III gives Reb Zalman's highly original exploration of *tzimtzum* as a powerful metaphor for Jewish Renewal, developed and supported with some of my own material.

The first draft of this work was written between 1999 and 2000, and was first published as a two-part article in *Spectrum: A Journal of Renewal Spirituality* (Vol. 2, Nos. 1 & 2) in 2006. It was later revised in 2013 and published as the first edition of *God Hidden, Whereabouts Unknown*. It was later revised again for a second edition, and once more for this present publication, adding the new material on the Ari Ha'Kodesh and translations in the appendices from the Rabbi Hayyim Vital, Rabbi Shneur Zalman of Liadi, and Rabbi Nahman of Bratzlav on *tzimtzum*. For his diligent proofreading of the manuscript, I am indebted to my student, Daniel Jami, who caught many errors.

— NETANEL MILES-YEPEZ
　　BOULDER, COLORADO
　　FEBRUARY 2ND, 2021

# PART I
## RABBI YITZHAK LURIA
### *THE HOLY LION*

# LIFE

RABBI YITZHAK LURIA, called *Ha'Ari,* 'the Lion' (an acrostic for *Ha'Elohi Rabbi Yitzhak,* 'the godly Rabbi Isaac') was born in Jerusalem in 1534. His father, Rabbi Shlomo Luria, was of an Ashkenazi family, while his mother was a Sefardi of the Frances clan. Rabbi Shlomo died young, and thus the Ari's mother was forced to take him to Egypt to live with her brother, Mordecai Frances, a successful tax-farmer. There, the Ari studied under the great Talmudic masters, Rabbi David Zimra (the Radbaz) and Rabbi Betzalel Ashkenazi, with whom the Ari collaborated on several halakhic works.

Later, the Ari married the daughter of his uncle, and began to engage in business, selling grain and various spices. In his private life, however, he studied *kabbalah,* the teachings of Jewish mysticism. In the early 1550s, or at least sometime before settling in S'fat (Safed) in 1569 or 1570, the Ari retired to a life of seclusion on an island, owned by his father-in-law near Cairo on the Nile, called Jazirat al-Rawda; tradition maintains that this seclusion lasted for seven years.

His kabbalistic studies seem to have focused primarily on the Zohar, the works of earlier kabbalists, and particularly on the writings of his contemporary, Rabbi Moshe Cordovero (1522-1570), the Ramak. It was probably during this period that he wrote the only work on *kabbalah* to come from his own pen, a commentary on the *Sifra d'Tzeniuta,* one of the most difficult sections of the Zohar. This work, however, betrays none of the highly original system of *kabbalah* that would later emerge from the Ari, and seems to be heavily influenced by the work of Cordovero.

In 1569, the Ari moved his family to S'fat where Rabbi Moshe Cordovero was leading a small community of kabbalists. There, he studied with the Ramak, "our teacher whose light may be prolonged," until the Ramak's death in the Fall of 1570. With the passing of Cordovero, the Ari emerged as his heir apparent, and the circle of S'fat kabbalists quickly drew close to him. It was then that he began to expound his own system of *kabbalah* (what is now called Lurianic Kabbalah) and seems to have gained the loyalty of his most famous disciple, Rabbi Hayyim Vital (1543-1620).

It is from Vital that we learn most of what we know of the Ari's life in S'fat. In addition to esoteric matters, it is known that the disciples also studied *halakhah* and the revealed Torah with the master. (Just a week before the Ari died, Vital reports that they had been studying Tractate Yevamot.) However, it should not be assumed that the Ari was a vocal public teacher in S'fat, though he did on occasion deliver homilies in S'fat's Ashkenazi synagogue; he preferred to teach his disciples in the open air on long walks through S'fat. On these walks he could point out the wonders of creation and demonstrate the living Torah. His last walk with them ended on July 15th (5th of Av), 1572, after two of the briefest and most seminal years in the history of *kabbalah*.

Most of what is known of the Ari's teaching is given in what is called the *Kitvei Ha'Ari*, the 'writings of the Ari,' which is actually a collection of various separate writings on the master's *kabbalah* by his disciples, most notably, Rabbi Hayyim Vital's *Etz Hayyim*, written down between 1573 and 1576. The crown jewel of the Ari's *kabbalah* is his threefold metaphor for the act of creation: *tzimtzum, shevirat ha'kelim,* and *tikkun.* Other notable teachings dealt with the use of mystical intentions *(kavvanot)* and the cycles of souls *(gilgulim).*

Sprinkled throughout various sources, we find a number of stories and anecdotes from the short life of the Ari. These are a few of our favorites . . .

# A Beginning

AFTER THE GREAT EXPULSION from golden Sefarad (Spain), a small Jewish community of refugees formed in the coastal city of S'fat and began to gather up the shards of a once beautiful vessel. Rabbi Moshe Cordovero, whose very name spoke of that lost land, was their guide. He gathered and ordered the 'fragments' by a new system, teaching his disciples the precise name of each broken piece. Then another man came silently among them and drank of the holy master's wisdom. When Reb Moshe passed from the earth a short time later, the silent one gathered up the neatly organized shards and spoke of how to renew the vessel.

# The Courtship of Hayyim Vital

S'FAT WAS THE BIRTHPLACE of Rabbi Hayyim Vital, who was accomplished in both *nigleh* and *nistar,* 'revealed' and 'hidden knowledge.' For a time, he studied under Rabbi Moshe Cordovero, but did not find in him a teacher for his soul, and soon he moved on to Damascus where he continued to pursue his own understanding of *kabbalah*. There he took on disciples, wrote a commentary on the Zohar, and began to settle into a high regard of himself.

When later he heard of Cordovero's passing, and of the great reputation of the Ari who had succeeded him, he was curious; yet he doubted if the young teacher had anything to teach him now. Still, his curiosity about the Ari was not so easily dismissed. It nudged him in quiet moments when he was away from his studies. He pushed it away. But soon it disturbed him even during his studies. Again, he pushed it away. Then, much to his horror, the Ari began to speak to Reb Hayyim in his dreams, urging him to come to S'fat so that he might teach him Torah.

Reb Hayyim was shaken by these dreams, but held firm, thinking—*What could I possibly learn from him?* Night after night the dream came again and again. Then, one day, after three months of such dreams, he labored over a portion of the Zohar, and try as he might, he could not understand it. Finally, he closed the book for the day, utterly frustrated. The next day he found the gates locked against a second passage, and against still another on a third day! Never before had such a thing happened to him. He was beside himself, saying, "First the dreams, and now I am blocked in my studies! . . . I'll see this master in S'fat and bring these passages to him. If he is unable to unlock them, then he is no greater than I, and I'll be rid of these dreams and frustrations!"

After a long journey, Reb Hayyim arrived in S'fat and called on the Ari without delay. To his amazement, the Ari received him at the door and treated him with such warmth that his own disdain pricked him. He was not to be so easily turned from his purpose, however; quickly he leapt to the subject of the impenetrable passages and challenged the Ari.

The Ari smiled, as if Reb Hayyim had offered him the most precious gift. This reaction completely surprised and confused Reb Hayyim, for he had made little effort to hide his contempt; and again he was met with sincere kindness. He sank into his seat as the Ari's eyes penetrated him, seeming to breathe in and absorb the zoharic rays which had touched Reb Hayyim. Then, closing his eyes, he began to reveal clearly and elegantly the first passage. Then, with eyes still closed, the second passage. For Reb Hayyim, it was as if he were moving down a river, a scene of tremendous beauty rising up to meet him on either side and passing him by. Then the vision faded as the Ari stopped. He brought his head down slightly and opened his eyes, saying, "Through this third passage, I am afraid you cannot pass; you have reached the limits of your understanding."

A sudden shame overwhelmed Reb Hayyim and he thought, *What have I done?* He thanked the Ari nervously and left in a hurry. In a whirlwind of thoughts and emotion, he went and found a room, falling on his bed sickened with his own pride, crying hot tears until they stopped in a firm decision.

He went to the *mikveh* and afterward returned to the Ari. "Master," he said, "please receive me; I wish to be your disciple."

After a long silence, the Ari replied, "I have long desired your presence, and have called you these many months. But the decision was not mine; it was yours. Your tears have done you credit and cleansed you to receive fresh garments. Come," he said, "these matters shall not be hidden from you any longer," and he embraced him.

Reb Hayyim then sat down to learn with two other disciples. However, each day he forgot what he had learned, until the master took him to Tiberius to drink from the Well of Miriam. After this, he retained whatever he learned.

## THE GREAT ASSEMBLY

REB HAYYIM VITAL TELLS: One day, I accompanied the Ari to the place where Rabbi Shimon bar Yohai had created and held the Greater Assembly. There, on the eastern side of the path, was a stone containing two large fissures. The Ari walked to the northern fissure and seated himself there. I turned to sit within the southern fissure. Then, the Ari explained that the northern fissure had been the place where Rabbi Shimon bar Yohai had sat, the southern had been the seat of Rabbi Abba, and Rabbi Elazar had seated himself at the foot of a nearby tree, which faced the two fissures. Some time after, he explained to me the significance of what had taken place, and it was then that I knew what he meant when he told me that I contained a spark of one of the members of the Greater Assembly.

## WHAT IS STILL LACKING?

ONCE, THE ARI SAID to his disciples: "Tomorrow, we'll take food and drink and go for a picnic; invite the rabbi who authored the book called *Weeping Voices*. Please do so immediately, for soon he'll proclaim a fast for himself and won't likely release himself from his vow once he has taken it."

As quickly as they were able, Reb Hayyim Vital, Reb Yosef ibn Tabul, and Reb Yisrael Sarug called upon the eminent rabbi and author. The rabbi, seeing the Ari's senior disciples coming to visit him, felt a twinge of pride and greeted them, "God's blessing upon you. Tell me, why have you left your master and come to me?"

Noting the prideful rabbi's intent, Reb Yisrael replied, "Rabbi, we have come because our master would like you to accompany us for a picnic tomorrow."

Concealing his disappointment, the rabbi said, "And why have you come today and not tomorrow?"

"Our master wished us to come before you imposed a fast on yourself, believing that once you had taken the vow, you would not likely release yourself."

At this, the rabbi scoffed, "Well, if this is the legendary perceptiveness of the great Ari, I am unimpressed."

Reb Hayyim responded, "Our master is what he is and shall be what he shall be; but I ask you again, respectfully, will you join us tomorrow?"

"I will join you," said the eminent rabbi.

In the morning, he met them as planned and they walked together out to the burial place of Rabbi Yehudah bar Ilai. Once there, they sat down to discourse on the Torah. Soon after, the Ari arrived and all rose up to greet him, except, that is, for the eminent rabbi, who simply nodded politely to him. For his part, the Ari seemed delighted to meet the noted rabbi and insisted that he be seated to his left. He then delivered a discourse to all present, recited Kaddish, and sat down.

Leaning to his left, noting the rabbis expression, the Ari asked, "My most learned colleague, were my words not pleasing to you?"

The rabbi responded with disinterest, "Not especially." But the Ari did not seem offended, inquiring further, "And why so?"

The rabbi then seized his opportunity: "I see many difficulties inherent in your discourse. For example, from the first, you expressed a view which was the reverse of that of Rabbi Shimon bar Yohai . . ." and he began to challenge the Ari on a number of small points.

Silence fell on the bewildered disciples. The Ari only shook his head gently, with just the hint of a smile. "Such a scholar as this," he said, "is to be praised, unlike some of you who agree with all that I say from the first." Then he turned to the flattered rabbi, "You are quite right; from where we are, it is difficult to look so far down the road; there may be difficulties and obstacles ahead to block us, as you have noted. But I have been there and have seen the path is clear. I will explain, and then we will eat; the others are hungry, and we too must eat, my friend"

Then, the Ari began to explain to the incredulous rabbi the clear path through all the difficulties that he had perceived and showed him the wonder of sight beyond the rounding turn of the Earth.

When the Ari had finished, the eminent rabbi, moved by this display of penetrating sight, trembled for the intense light of Torah that had been revealed to him, and he stood up, saying, "Master, it is better that I sit at your feet, for I am humbled and embarrassed to say that a moment ago I considered you lower than the least of my students; but now I know that the spirit of the Lord is in you."

The Ari then lifted him up again, and they all ate and drank joyfully.

Later, they walked home, and as they were about to take leave of one another, the Ari looked to the eminent rabbi and said, "Rest well." But the rabbi returned, "May we both sleep well. I shall not, however, until you prescribe a penance for my soul, for I have dishonored a servant of the Holy One."

The Ari said to him, "Rest you well," and entered his own home.

The next day, the rabbi appeared again before him, still more stricken than the night before, "Rabbi, I could find no rest the whole night. You must give me a penance to perform. How shall I bear what I have done any longer? Please, give me a penance!"

The Ari responded, "Who am I that I should give such a one as you a penance? And were I to give it to you *again,* you would be hard pressed to honor it."

In his eagerness, the rabbi pressed on, "Were it to be one of the four deaths set by the court, I should be ready to die with joy."

The master looked to the heavens and then to the earth and said, "I call the heavens and earth to witness my love for this man." He then lifted his eyes to the rabbi and said slowly, "Now, hear me, my friend, *rest well.* Though you desire to purge the sin from your body through many privations, I tell you to refrain from your fasting and each day eat a fine fatted fowl, meditating on the delight of the Torah."

Then he embraced the Ari and kissed him, and went out healed.

Not long after, in gratitude, he invited the Ari and his disciples to a great feast, which would also be attended by the *ga'on,* his 'excellency' Rabbi Moshe Galante, who was among the most celebrated sages of that generation.

On being invited by his dear friend, the *ga'on* had readily accepted, but asked in curiosity, "What, my friend, is so exceptional about this day that you will make such a feast?"

The rabbi replied, "Today, my heart is healed, and I have invited the healer to dine with you and I at a feast in his honor."

"And who is this healer of hearts?" Rabbi Moshe asked.

"The rabbi, Yitzhak Ashkenazi."

The *ga'on* sat back with interest, "Well now, I have heard of him. Have you tested him and found him in the word of the Lord?"

The rabbi answered, "I have tested him . . . and found myself wanting." He then went on to recount the entire episode to the *ga'on,* who listened with evident amazement, finally saying, "Then it is a *mitzvah* to attend this feast!"

The day of the feast, the Ari and his disciples arrived at the time they were summoned and praised their host for his hospitality. They were seated according to the good rabbi's wishes and fell into an easy conversation. Then, as Rabbi Moshe Galante entered, the Ari rose immediately, followed closely by his disciples. Suddenly, he realized that he was seated at the head of the table and quickly entreated the *ga'on* to take the head of the table.

The good rabbi then told him, "But, holy Rabbi, you are the guest of honor."

The Ari, seeing no way out, acquiesced to the honor, but said, "While I can accept that this dinner should be for me, you will understand that I cannot, however, sit at the head of any table where Rabbi Moshe Galante is seated lower."

Finally, the *ga'on* sat down at the head of the table, and they found joy in one another's company until the feast was ended.

The next morning, the *ga'on* knocked at the Ari's door, and the Ari (opening the door) was perplexed for the second time in as many days. Here, the *ga'on*, Rabbi Moshe Galante, had come to his door, when he should have summoned the Ari had he wanted to see him.

The Ari said hurriedly, "I am ashamed that you have put yourself through the trouble to call on me. I would have come to you. Please, come in and rest a while. What can I do for you, Ga'on?"

Then Rabbi Moshe said to him, "I have come for a penance for my soul." Looking weary, the Ari knelt beside him and looked at the *ga'on* searchingly, saying softly, "Ga'on, what am I, and what is my life that I should set a penance for your excellency?"

Then, the *ga'on* said, "If you won't prescribe a penance, then may I ask that you look upon my forehead and tell me what you see?"

"You may."

"Then I ask you to do so."

The Ari looked and immediately looked down and said, "Your honesty is suspect."

The words struck at the heart of the *ga'on,* and he could say nothing. He hurried to his home, took off his clothing, put on sackcloth and ashes, and mourned for this suspicion on his honesty, far be it from the truth!

"How shall I hide my shame, given that I am called a judge here in S'fat."

He sobbed until there were no more tears and exhaustion took him.

Now, amidst this commotion, his household was terribly upset and brought water to revive him. He drank a little and called his assistant to assemble all of his workers and servants, women and men, before him.

Within a half-an-hour, they had all entered and were shocked to find the *ga'on* in sackcloth. They were still more shocked to hear the sorrowful *ga'on* entreat them, "Please, listen to me, and do as I ask. Each of you, give me a full account of what I owe you."

They all looked at one another until finally one spoke up, "Ga'on, not one of us keeps an account, for you are fair at all times. It is known to us all that the money you give grants a special blessing, so that we always have enough food, drink, and clothing. So what account need we keep for you? There is no knowing what the totals may be!"

The *ga'on* then shook his head gravely and said, "Surely, you are speaking your truth; but you must understand that there is in this world both judgment and justice, and thus, I sit in this manner before you. My heart longs to be true, and there is yet something amiss. Now, I ask you to henceforth be very exacting in your accounts with me, for that is how I must have it." Then, he called his assistant to bring a plate full of coin and to set it on the table. The assistant did so, and the *ga'on* said to them, "This is for past misdealing—take what you wish," and he turned to leave. But the same man who had spoken insisted again, "But master, how shall we know, having no account?"

Then he said to them, "Let us make an agreement; take what you wish and declare with a good conscience: 'I have received all that is due to me from this day, and if it be that more was due to me, I forgive you freely.' And I will say likewise."

Immediately, they each came forward and forgave him; but none took a single coin, except for one woman who took two piasters. When he urged her to take more, she refused and departed quickly.

The *ga'on* rushed to his bedchamber, dressed, and departed to the home of the Ari. But the Ari met him on the way this time and asked quickly, "Why the haste, Ga'on?"

The *ga'on* embraced him and said, "Is the matter resolved, my friend?"

The Ari said, "It is all past, my lord."

"Is there then no more atonement required? What was it that was hidden from my eyes?"

"Ga'on," the Ari replied, "it concerned the woman who took the two piasters. She, being a weaver of fine cloth, was due more in wages than the other weavers;

you failed to make this distinction and paid her as the weavers of coarse cloth."

The *ga'on* kissed him in gratitude and made a blessing upon him, and thereafter held the Ari in great esteem.

## THE ARI'S TORAH

ONE DAY, AS THE Ari rested in his mid-day nap, his disciple, Reb Avraham Brukhim, was watching him from the adjoining room. After a few moments, Reb Avraham noticed something odd; the Ari's lips seemed to be moving as he slept. Thinking perhaps the master was awake, or, God forbid, sick, he entered the room very quietly and leaned near.

Now, the Ari did not appear to be unwell, but neither was he awake. So a great curiosity overcame Reb Avraham, thinking, "What heavenly Torah would come from the master's dreams!" So he knelt down with the greatest care and inclined his ear close to the Ari's mouth; but he could hear only the faintest whisper. Suddenly aware that the Ari's eyes were open, he stood up very quickly, confounded by a mixture of fright and shame.

"Forgive me, master!," he said imploringly. "At first, I thought perhaps something was amiss, but when I found that it was not, and saw a *tzaddik*'s lips moving, I leaned close to listen."

The Ari laughed a father's laugh, and said with a smile and a sigh, "Avraham, I wish I could tell you the secret lore my soul received in my short rest. But Heaven and Earth will witness that were I to have eighty years with you, I could not tell you all of what I have just learned of Ba'alam's ass."

With open-eyed sincerity, Reb Avraham then asked what all the disciples had been wondering, "Why don't you set this wisdom down in a book, then?"

The Ari sighed again, "Alas, I do not think it possible —all things as so inter-woven; how shall I separate this wholeness? Even when I open my mouth to speak, the great seas rush from the fountain spout and I must purse my lips and let the great waters trickle from my mouth. But the pressure is great within! A little more and you might drown, like a babe choked by an overabundance of milk. The trickle, however, forms droplets that you may receive without any loss. From my mouth to yours is this wisdom given, gently and in just the right measure. But how so with a book? Rather, let each of you write what Torah you have imbibed from me."

So they did according to his word. Lurianic strands from the great fabric, and drops from the seas they each put in their books—Reb Hayyim Vital, Reb Yisrael Sarug, Reb Moshe Yonah, and Reb Yosef ibn Tabul— all with a unique emphasis, seeds from the master.

## HALLAHS IN THE ARK

AT THE BEGINNING OF the sixteenth century, Jews who had been expelled from Spain tried to settle all over. Some traveled to Salonika in Greece, some to France, some to Germany. One man, whose name was Jacobo, and his wife Esperanza, settled in S'fat, the city where *kabbalah* flourished.

When Jacobo came to S'fat, the only language he spoke was Spanish, so that when he went to the synagogue and listened to the rabbi's sermons, he did not really understand everything he heard.

One Shabbat, the rabbi, who was sixty years old, gave a sermon in which he mentioned that, in the Holy Temple, God was offered twelve loaves of bread each week before Shabbat. Jacobo did not exactly understand everything about that sermon, but when he came home he said to 'Speranza excitedly, "Next week, Friday morning, I want you to bake twelve loaves of *pan de Dios* for me to bring to the synagogue! The old *rabino* said that God likes to have special bread for Shabbat, and I know that you bake the best hallah in the whole country! So next Shabbat, I am going to bring God some of your hallah!"

That week Esperanza baked especially good hallahs. She kneaded the dough until it was extra smooth, and put all her good intentions into the dough, along with the special ingredients. Then, Friday morning, Jacobo wrapped them all up in a nice white tablecloth and took them to the synagogue.

When he got to the synagogue, Jacobo looked around to make sure that no one was watching, went up to the Holy Ark, kissed the curtain in front of the Ark, and said, *"Señor Dios,* I bring you twelve hallahs that my 'Speranza baked. She is really a good baker, and I hope you will like her hallah. Tomorrow morning, when they take out the *Sefer Torah,* I am going to look inside the Ark, and I expect to see every crumb gone, because my 'Speranza really bakes good hallah!"

Then he opened the Ark, put the twelve hallahs inside, arranged them neatly, said, *"¡Buen apetito!"* and then closed the Ark, kissed the curtain, stepped back seven steps, and walked out of the synagogue very happy that God would have such good hallahs to eat.

A few minutes later, the *shammash*, or synagogue attendant, came in with his broom, talking to God. "Seven weeks already with no pay! I'm cleaning up the synagogue, and dear Lord, you know I only want one thing in my life—I just want to be here in your house. I don't want another job; I just want to be the *shammash* here! But dear Lord, my children are getting so hungry. I know you can do miracles. Please make a miracle for me; I need a miracle so bad. I am going to open up the Holy Ark and I know you will make a miracle; I will find something inside that will help me and my family!"

He walks over, opens the *Aron Kodesh*, the Holy Ark, and sure enough, there is the miracle. "I knew it! I knew it! The *Ribbono shel Olam* never forsakes anyone."

Taking the twelve hallahs in his arms, he makes his way home. Once home, he announces, "Tonight we will have two hallahs for the Shabbat table! In the morning, after davening, we will have two hallahs. For the Third Meal, we will have two more hallahs, and then there will be one hallah for each day of the week! And next week we will see what happens."

The very next morning, Jacobo and Esperanza came to synagogue (Esperanza going upstairs to the women's section), and both waited anxiously to see what would happen. *Will the hallahs still be there when the Holy Ark is opened? Or will God have really liked the hallah and taken every crumb?*

When the old rabbi opened the Holy Ark and reached in to take out the Torah, Jacobo, who had snuck up behind the rabbi, peeked in and saw that the hallahs were gone! "Oh, *Barukh Ha'Shem!* Thank God!"

He winked up at his wife, Esperanza, and went back to his seat.

The next week, Esperanza got the best ingredients she could find. Thursday evening she started making the dough. Friday morning she baked them. Fresh and delicious, Jacobo wrapped them, took them to the synagogue, and left them in the *Aron Kodesh* just like the week before.

A few minutes later the synagogue attendant came and picked up his miracle hallahs.

This scene repeated itself every week.

Over time, the synagogue attendant realized that if he came too early, or if he stayed to watch the *Aron Kodesh,* no miracle occurred. He learned that he had to rely on God and wait until about ten o'clock on Friday morning for his miracle hallahs.

Thirty years passed this way. One Friday, as Jacobo was bringing the hallahs to the Holy Ark, he prayed to God, *"Señor Dios,* my poor 'Speranza is getting arthritis. Her fingers are not so good anymore for kneading the hallah dough. If you don't like the lumps in the hallah, you better fix my 'Speranza's hands. I hope you enjoy them anyway!" Jacobo left the twelve hallahs, kissed the hem of the curtain over the Ark, walked his seven customary steps backward, and—*Aargh!!*—the long bony hand of the old rabbi, now ninety years old, grabbed poor frightened Jacobo by the neck!

"What did you just do?" asked the rabbi angrily.

"I brought God his *pan de Dios,* his weekly hallah!"

"Why would you do that?"

"Thirty years ago, *Rabino,* you gave a sermon about *pan de Dios* in the Holy Temple, and ever since I've brought God hallah."

"Are you crazy? God doesn't eat!"

*"Señor Rabino,"* Jacobo said, "you may be a rabbi, and you may know lots of things better than me; but God does eat!"

"What do you mean?"

"For thirty years, every crumb disappears from the Holy Ark!"

Curious now, the old rabbi pulled Jacobo aside to hide in the back of the synagogue. "Let's see what happens," said the rabbi.

A few minutes, the synagogue attendant enters and stands before the Ark, saying, "Dear Lord, I don't know what it is, but something is going wrong with the angels up there. Lately the hallah has been very lumpy. For thirty years I've been sustained by your angels, so I can't complain; but I just thought you might like to know. Maybe you can ask the angels to knead the dough a little better? Thank you anyways."

He then steps up to the Holy Ark, takes out the hallahs, closes it, walks back a few steps, and—*Aargh!*— "You terrible man!" yells the old rabbi, shaking the poor *shammash* by the neck. "On account of you, this man, Jacobo, has sinned the great sin of anthropomorphism! What do you think you are doing!?"

"Listen," the synagogue attendant explained, "you don't pay me. This is my *parnassa,* my living. Every week God makes a miracle for me!"

Soon, both the attendant and Jacobo are crying, one because he knew he would not find any more hallahs in the Ark, and the other because he had thought he was making God happy. Then the old rabbi began to cry too—"How could such a terrible thing come from my good sermon? I never said God eats! It goes against what the Rambam says—God has no body! God doesn't eat. What terrible Jews I have in my congregation!"

Just then, Rabbi Hayyim Vital, the chief disciple of the Ari, came in to the synagogue.

"My master, the *Ari Ha'Kodesh,*" he said, "wants all of you to come to his house, now."

So, Jacobo, the poor synagogue attendant, and the old rabbi all went to the Ari's house, and the Ari said to the old rabbi—"Go home, make sure your will is in order, because you will die before Shabbat. Thirty years ago, your time was up; but you were given thirty more years to live because, since the destruction of the Holy Temple, God has not had so much joy on Friday mornings since beginning to watch what goes on in your synagogue between these two men. On Friday mornings, God calls all the angels together to watch Jacobo bringing the hallahs, and the *shammash* coming to get them, God getting all the credit. For this reason, God told the Angel of Death to leave you be until this day. Now that you have spoiled God's joy, go home and get ready, so they can bury your body before Shabbat."

Then, the Ari turned to Jacobo and said, "Now that you know who has been eating your hallah, it is going to be a little bit harder; but I want you to believe with perfect faith that if you bring the hallahs directly to the *shammah,* God will be no less pleased."

## AN ALIYAH TO JERUSALEM

ONE LATE AFTERNOON AS the Shabbat approached, the Ari gathered his disciples to him. "Prepare for a journey," he told them, "for we will spend Shabbat in Yerushalayim (Jerusalem)." When the disciples heard this, they were amazed and bewildered.

One of them protested, "Master, how shall we make such a long journey with *erev* Shabbat only minutes away? Surely, we will not be traveling on Shabbat?" he asked fearfully.

The Ari smiled kindly and explained, "Time, space, and motion are but expressions of the limitations imposed by the physical body on the soul. However, when the soul leads the body, these limits cease to exist. So let us ascend to Yerushalayim, for our corporeal bodies have ceased to limit our souls."

Thus, intoning chants of love and longing, the Ari and his disciples arrived in Jerusalem in time to greet the Shabbat herself.

Soon after, at the age of thirty-eight, on the 5th of Av, 1572, the Ari completed his task on Earth and ascended to the place awaiting him in *Gan Eden.*

# PART II
## PARADIGM SHIFT &
## THE DIVINE CONTRACTION

# TZIMTZUM

*TZIMTZUM*, OR 'CONTRACTION,' is the first movement in the holy kabbalist's, Rabbi Yitzhak Luria's, stunning myth of Creation. Indeed, it is Luria who, steeped in the mystical teachings of the *Zohar*, actually restores a truly mythological perspective to Judaism, teaching us . . .

*Know this . . .*
*Before Emanations*
*And Creations,*
*A Simple Light*
*Filled all of*
*Existence.*

*All was Full*
*With Simplicity,*
*With Infinite Light.*

*No beginning,*
*No end;*
*All was One*
*Uniform Light.*

*Now, the Will*
*To create Worlds*
*And Emanations*
*Emerged.*

*Now, the Infinite*
*Contracted Self*
*In the Center*
*Of Its Light*

*Withdrawing*
*From that Center*
*To the sides*
*Surrounding,*
*Leaving an*
*Empty Space,*
*A Void.[1]*

That is to say, *tzimtzum* was and is a self-contraction of the light of divinity, withdrawing from a point at its 'center,' making a space in which creation might have a limited autonomy in the midst of God's overwhelming presence.

What is most interesting about the Ari's imagery is that the infinite light contracts *away* from the center, creating a womb-like space, leading us to believe that God is somehow 'pregnant' with creation; God is, as the *kabbalah* teaches, *sovev kol almin*, 'surrounding all worlds.'

For the generations that followed the Ari, his concept of *tzimtzum* was a breath of fresh air, creating

---

1 Hayyim Vital, *Liqqutim Hadashim*, 17-23.

a new vitality in kabbalistic speculation. But it was also a source of controversy, as a variety of interpretations battled for supremacy. Depending on one's interpretation of *tzimtzum*, the ideas of God it reveals vary radically. In the *Tikkunei Zohar*, we read . . .

> *You are Most High*
> *Of the Most High*
> *Most Hidden*
> *Of the Undisclosed;*
> *No thought-scheme*
> *May grasp You*
> *In any way.*

That is to say, God (or God's essence) is truly beyond our ability to conceive. But, as *theo-tropic* beings, ever yearning for and growing toward God, we are continually searching for God's "hidden" and "undisclosed" essence.

What does that tell us? *That our idea of God is less about God than about our own capacity to conceive of God.* Thus, it follows that our 'God-concepts' have evolved through the centuries like all our other concepts, even as the words delivered to the prophet Malachi have remained true—"I am *Y-H-V-H*, I have not changed." (Mal. 3:6)

Yet, to understand this idea fully, we must first understand something about the nature of paradigm shift.

# Epochs &

## Reality-Maps

AN EPOCH IS A new beginning, a fluid period of transition, establishing 'new gods' for a new era. In the long history of consciousness, the human community has collectively experienced many such epochs. They are significant periods of change in the general character of our awareness.

In such liquid moments of vague beginning, a sleeper awakens. The sleeper is not one human being, but a discontent seeded through an entire generation, or a series of generations. Their waking-up is gradual—light begins to flood through the eyelids, and an awareness of time and need cause a general stir through the body. It does not happen in a single moment; it is a waking-sequence progressing from the slow and blunted awareness experienced at first light to the deft precision and clear head of mid-morning. But the discontented of that epochal period awaken to more than an empty belly; they also find they have a taste for something they have never before experienced.

The epoch occurs when the efficacy of the then dominant 'reality-map'—that system of shared religious and cultural beliefs by which we orient ourselves in all situations—begins to break down, initiating a process of shifting from one paradigm to another, more viable, and better able to sustain its constituents in a new situation.

The epochal period is simply a natural, adaptive, evolutionary process for ensuring our collective survival. It is a tool for reshaping the landscape of our collective mental and spiritual frontiers, creating a new reality-map to replace the one that preceded it.

The new reality-map is a 'guide for the perplexed,' as well as a contemporary container for the *magisterium*, or collected knowledge of a tradition. It is a kind of oracle to which the spiritual seeker can bring their confusion. It listens, understands, and tells them, *'This is how it is; this is as it should be,'* and the seeker is comforted. But it is also a container for ideas whose shape represents but a stage of development in the whole history of ideas. It speaks to a particular world-situation, to the culture of the time, and it is in accord with the knowledge of the day. It is timely, and thus can easily handle questions from the world-view of which it is a part. But it is not exclusive to the exact moment in history which gave birth to it either; it is built with some 'give' in its sides, so that it can grow with the people it serves.

And yet, as with every time-born thing, a moment comes when the container has stretched to the breaking-point and bursts, loosing again the previously contracted primal-flow. The cycle is completed and one returns to the epochal period.

Of course, this is an abstracted and intellectual way of talking about the process of paradigm shift. Most people experience the death throes and birth pangs of the shifting process as difficult and painful. For when a reality-map ceases to function and serve the needs of its constituents, they quite naturally feel betrayed by it. After all, bringing their most profound feelings and questions to it, they are met with what seem like mere platitudes. Asking for the *'all'* that it once provided to those who went before them, they receive barely enough to fill their mouths.

But the answers they are getting are not mere platitudes, as they seem; they are only the answers of another time, another situation, another paradigm. For the reality-map they are addressing was built to address the needs of others, long ago. What was once responsive and innovative is now clumsy, struggling even to understand the questions being asked of it. The Copernican Revolution could not have been conceived by the Ptolemaic reality-map that came before it. Thus, the generation living at the end of a paradigm reaches out to its reality-map, seeking a genuine response, and is disappointed to receive what seems like a condescending recapitulation of old 'truths' and answers from the 'good old days.' The situation is untenable, and the utter frustration of it is what eventually gives rise to the dynamic period of conception between paradigms.

Thus, the failure to communicate with a new generation drives the creative flow to conceive of a new and more responsive reality-map; the tragedy of the 'communication gap' turns out to be but the birth pangs of a new paradigm, the catalyst for a spiritual revolution. As the boundary-pushing artist Robert Irwin put it, "Revolutions don't cause change; change causes revolutions."[2]

These epochal days are precisely those 'interesting times' in which the old Chinese curse wishes you to live; that is to say—*full of difficulties.* For even though it

---

2 Lawrence Weschler, *Seeing is Forgetting the Name of the Thing One Sees,* 201.

will be clear to some that the old paradigm has become irrelevant, its influence will live on in others, others who will hold all the more tightly to it, precisely because of all the changes in their world. In the epochal period, the body of the slouched and breathless king has not yet yielded the throne, but nor has a clear successor emerged to clear away the ruined body and its influence. One is reminded of Finnegan in James Joyce's *Finnegans Wake*, who himself represents a passing paradigm. After suffering a bad fall while drunk, his comrades think he is dead and decide to hold an Irish wake for him. Of course, he is not dead, but merely unconscious, and soon rises from his coffin during the festivities, only to be held down by his reveling friends who insist that he "rest in peace," seeing as his successor has already arrived to replace him!

So the way ahead often seems blocked by the unyielding 'dead weight' of the past. And yet, things are not as hopeless or as static as they seem. For the old 'king' is dying, and the land is being saturated with a new and creative vitality from his 'body.' Just as humus is the life of the soil, the decaying body of the old king, the old reality-map, gives impetus to its emerging successor. At that moment, a ferment of syncretistic-creation suddenly arises, guided by a teleological pull toward a new paradigm. It is a period of radical experimentation and rich cross-fertilization; the empirical-experiential is raised above the legal-rational, and the once rigid forms become fluid again, opening tradition to revitalizing influences. The memory of the old is re-interpreted and elaborated to suit the needs of a new age, a new spiritual landscape. And in this way, another reality-map is born.

One of the questions we will explore here is—how has our concept of God (in relation to Luria's *tzimtzum*) been affected by the changing of reality-maps? For the idea of *tzimtzum,* it turns out, is useful for showing just how the shifting occurs, its relevance is to Jewish Renewal, and where that renewal is taking us.

Borrowing language from Western Astrology, we will speak about the various reality-maps Judaism has seen in terms of four discrete eras: Taurus, the age of polytheism (4,000 B.C.E to 2,000 B.C.E.); Aries, the age of deism (2,000 B.C.E. to 1 C.E.); Pisces, the age of theism (1 C.E. to the Present); and Aquarius, the age of pantheism (our future for the next 2,000 years).

# ARIES —

## DEISTIC TZIMTZUM

GERSHOM SCHOLEM BELIEVED that the Holy Ari's concept of *tzimtzum* was probably derived from an obscure passage in a 13th-century treatise speculating about God's creative activity . . .

> How did he produce and create this world? Like a man who gathers in and contracts *[m'tzamtzem]* his breath *[...]*, so that the smaller might contain the larger, so He contracted His light into a hand's breadth, according to His own measure, and the world was left in darkness.[3]

Still earlier, in the sayings of the 3rd-century sages found in the Midrash, the word *m'tzamtzem* is used to speak of God as contracting and concentrating the divine presence *(Shekhinah)* into a single point between the wings of the cherubim *(k'ruvim)* on the Ark of Testimony in the Holy of Holies *(kadosh kodashim)*.[4] But even this usage represents a theistic viewpoint from the 3rd-century C.E., and not the deistic view that would have existed in Torah.[5]

---

3 Gershom Scholem, *Kabbalah*, 129.
4 *Midrash Rabbah*, Shemot Rabbah on Exodus 25:22.
5 Not to be confused with the popular deism of the 17th and 18th-centuries, which compared God to a 'clockmaker,' who creates the world and sets all things in motion, but who takes no further part in creation.

Although the Torah does not itself speak of *tzimtzum*, it is nevertheless the source interpreted in the *midrash* above. So let us examine the 'ground level' in Torah and see how this 'event' would have been understood in the deistic view of the patriarchal age.

In Exodus 25:22, God says to Moses . . .

I will meet you there, and will speak with you from above the cover, from between the cherubim on the Ark of Testimony, concerning the children of Israel.

At that time, it is almost certain that God is believed to have actually located there, in space and time, between the wings of the cherubim on the Ark of Testimony. From that place, God would communicate with Moses. That is to say, God was thought to be 'mobile' and capable of 'occupying' physical spaces.

The deist conceived of God as an anthropomorphic, anthropopathic *Other* moving *ad libitum* through time and space, like a territorial overlord. In this model, God occupies and travels from discrete space to discrete space, and places are said to become holy because God has been present in them at one time or another.

The Bible gives us many examples of this deist notion of a God who comes down from elsewhere. In Genesis 18:21, God says, "Let me go *down* and see" what the people in Sodom are doing. But if God comes "down" to us, where is God the rest of the time? *Beyond the beyond.* When that *beyond the beyond* breaks through and descends into our space, we say, 'It lowers Itself.' God *contracts* the divine self in order "to see what is going on in heaven and on earth" (Ps. 113). For it is not only earth that is low to God, but also heaven!

God, in this reality-map, is 'totally other'—*totaliter aliter*—coming from an altogether different sphere of reality. Thus, God tells us, "Your thoughts are not like my thoughts" (Isa. 55:8), and, "To whom can you liken me so that I would compare?" (Isa. 40:25). God is completely different and superior to us, and it is our inferiority that obligates us to God.

So it is clear that the *tzimtzum* of God in the deist paradigm refers to a literal contraction of God (or God's essence) between the wings of the cherubim on the Ark of Testimony. Thus, after receiving the Torah in the wilderness, Israel built a tabernacle to God: "They shall make me a sanctuary, and I shall dwell among them" (Ex. 25:8). And so, as God contracts and occupies one space, God is also absent from another; and those spaces that God occupies become sacralized by God's presence in them.

# PISCES —
## THEISTIC TZIMTZUM

THE THEIST SEES GOD as the great *anima mundi*, the oversoul of the life of the universe, whose arena is time and not space. From the theistic viewpoint, God no longer moves in space, but is understood to influence and enter *time* through the power of the divine will. God, the greatest spirit, creates matter simply by saying the word, *"Be!"* and abracadabra—*ibra k'dibra*, Aramaic for 'created as the word is spoken'—the words of that fiat enter form and keep it in being. God lives outside of our sphere and governs it from above. God no longer *descends* into our sphere, but moves servant-powers to establish the divine will here on earth.

In the Middle Ages, people began to say that God created the world *ex nihilo*, or *mi'ain*, 'from nothing.' That is to say, there was nothing in existence before God spoke the word, "Be!" bringing the universe into being.

This divine ability is indicated in God's private name, *Y-H-V-H*, the final three letters of which—*Heh-Vav-Heh*—mean, 'to be.' If you put the letter *Yod* in front of them, the meaning adjusts to, 'the one who causes being,' or the 'being-maker.'

So God says, "Be!" and we are told, "the heavens were made with the word of God." That is to say, everything is created and sustained by God's word, the word being the most essential power that can be imagined in theism.

In contrast to the deistic example from Torah, which says that God will place the divine self between the wings of the cherubim, it says in Rashi's theistic commentary on this same passage . . .

> When God spoke to Moses, the *voice* would come from heaven, and from between the wings of the cherubim would emanate to the place where Moses stood in the outer chamber of the Tabernacle.

In this paradigm, the sages shy away from the many anthropomorphisms used in Torah, preferring instead to speak of God's 'voice' or 'speech,' God's 'glory,' or the 'divine presence,' the *Shekhinah*. Thus, Onkelos the Proselyte, who translated the Torah from Hebrew into Aramaic, translates the verse from Exodus 25:22, "I will meet with you there," which seems to indicate that God will physically place the divine self between the wings of the cherubim, as, "I will cause my *word* to meet you, and I will *speak* with you."

In the theistic paradigm, it is no longer acceptable to regard God as some sort of anthropomorphic 'superhuman.' Thus, Onkelos and others attempt to rescue God from this unsophisticated viewpoint with new translations and novel interpretations of scripture. For this work, Maimonides, the great 12th-century philosopher and legal authority, expresses his gratitude, saying . . .

> Onkelos the Proselyte was perfect in the Hebrew and Syrian languages and directed his effort toward the abolition of the belief in God's corporeality. Hence he interprets in accordance with its meaning

every attribute that Scripture predicates of God and that might lead toward the belief in corporeality.[6]

According to Maimonides, the doctrine of the incorporeality or immateriality of God does not contradict the Torah in its use of anthropomorphisms, nor is it a mere projection upon it from the theistic paradigm. He demonstrates this by elucidating the finer points of meaning in the Hebrew words, 'image' *(tzelem)*, 'likeness' *(demut)*, and 'form' *(to'ar)*, which, when properly understood, actually justify the idea of the incorporeality of God . . .

> People have thought that in the Hebrew language *image* denotes the shape and configuration of a thing. This supposition led them to the pure doctrine of the corporeality of God, on account of His saying: "Let us make man in our image, after our likeness" (Gen. 1:26). For they thought that God has a man's form, I mean his shape and configuration.[7]

Nevertheless, Maimonides tells us that the proper way to designate 'form' in Hebrew is *to'ar*, "which is the shape and configuration of a thing." This word is never applied to God in Torah. The Hebrew word applied to God, *tzelem*, or 'image,' actually refers to the "intellectual apprehension" of God.[8]

---

6 Isadore Twersky, ed., *A Maimonides Reader*, 251. Also Moses Maimonides, tr. Shlomo Pines, *The Guide of the Perplexed*, 57.
7 Ibid., 246. Also Maimonides, *The Guide of the Perplexed*, 21.
8 Ibid., 246-47. Also Maimonides, *The Guide of the Perplexed*, 21-22.

Having shown that the Torah is fully in accord with the doctrine of the incorporeality of God, Maimonides goes on to show that all the instances of speaking positively of God's attributes in Torah are merely devices to deny any "imperfection" in God. Thus, he writes, "Of this thing we say that it exists, the meaning being that its non-existence is impossible."[9] And if we say, "God is one," it is simply to exclude "multiplicity."[10] Likewise, attributes such as 'omnipotence' and 'omniscience' are but the denial of 'impotence' and 'ignorance' in God. In this way, the veil of misconception is torn asunder instance-by-instance; and in the end, Maimonides tells us that we can know nothing of God except the fact of God's existence.[11]

According to Maimonides, nothing is *actually* 'predicated' or attributed to God in the positive attributions made in scripture. They are merely there to deny the opposite, to deny that God has any deficiency whatsoever.

This argument followed that of the Greek Neo-Platonists who used negative statements about God to express a positive content. However, it is clear that Maimonides' God is the God of Torah, and his was not an attempt to mold the Neo-Platonic idea onto biblical material, but simply to express the true reality, as he saw it, with greater clarity.[12]

For Maimonides, this was no mere philosophical sublimation of the idea of God, to tame irrational

---

9 Maimonides, *The Guide of the Perplexed*, 135.
10 Julius Guttmann, tr. David W. Silverman, *Philosophies of Judaism: The History of Jewish Philosophy from Biblical Times to Franz Rosenzweig*, 183.
11 Ibid., 183.
12 Ibid., 183-84.

religion, but a duty of religious observance to achieve a purer understanding of monotheism. For him, as for the Neo-Platonists, God is truly beyond comprehension. Indeed, God is *God* precisely by being *beyond* comprehension. Nevertheless, Maimonides' God is still the creator God, and thus a personal God.[13]

---

13 Ibid., 180, 186.

# From Infinity
## to Finitude

PHILOSOPHY IN THE theistic paradigm had drawn a sharp line between what was knowable about God and what was not. God could still be addressed with our concerns and petitions, but the sages realized that talking *about* God was a very different proposition. God had to be spoken of as both 'infinite' and 'transcendent.' But when these ideas were married to the words of Torah, new questions arose. For instance—how did an infinite and transcendent God create the universe? How could the finite possibly proceed from the infinite?

In philosophy, a logical inconsistency causes the whole system to fall apart; so these questions needed to be answered. It is also important to remember that infinity is not a matter of numbers; you cannot say 'Infinity minus one equals a zillion.' Even if you were to subtract a billion, it would not matter; it is infinity regardless of what you try to take out of it.

Having established God as infinite, as the *Pleroma*, the 'fullness of the utter fullness,' happening on all wavelengths, how could one possibly say that this somehow became finite? How are we to reconcile this idea with that of a finite universe of which we are a part? How are we to understand the oneness of God in the face of the multiplicity of creation?

To deal with this logical inconsistency, some kabbalists proposed a theory of 'intermediate steps' between the infinite God and finite creation. The thinking was that by describing the very subtle transitional steps leading from the unmanifest into manifestation, the problem is somehow solved. But this 'solution' does not solve the problem at all; the question of just when the infinite becomes finite remains unanswered; for no matter how many steps are added, and no matter how subtle they are, there is still a point at which infinity must become finite—*infinite* is *infinite* and *finite* is *finite*, and never the twain shall meet.[14]

This is why the Holy Ari's concept of *tzimtzum* is so important. *Tzimtzum* is a 'break,' or a 'gap,' between the creator and the created. Before creation, he tells us, there is only God's infinite oneness. But when it arose in God's will to create the finite universe, God, as it were, contracted infinity away from a point, creating a spherical space, a Void *(halal)* in which 'finitude' could exist.

The question is—how do we interpret this 'gap'? Are we to understand *tzimtzum* as a literal or a metaphorical 'contraction'? The literalist interpreters were on the front-line in the defense of the old theistic notion of God; whereas the metaphorical interpreters proposed a new, pantheistic paradigm or reality-map.

The literal interpreters believed that God actually removed the divine essence from that spherical space, creating a Void that is, as it were, *devoid* of God's essence, and in which creation could take place. Thus, it is only

---

14 See Noson Gurary, *Chasidism: Its Development, Theology, and Practice,* 67-68, on Moshe Cordovero's teaching of 'intermediate steps.'

from 'outside' the Void that God 'oversees' the creation process.

As a proof for this view, the theists argued that, if we were to interpret *tzimtzum* metaphorically, we would be forced to conclude that God's essence could actually be found in such 'unworthy places' as garbage dumps, and in such 'lowly things' as human waste—not to mention, things that are not kosher. This, of course, was unacceptable in their view. That is to say, the pantheistic, metaphorical interpretation of *tzimtzum* means that God's essence is still *here* in this space, even in such unworthy places and lowly things, because *tzimtzum* is really only the 'wool pulled over our eyes.'

Because the theists could not accept this disturbing possibility—but still had to deal with the zoharic statement, "No place is devoid of God"[15]—they were forced to come up with an alternate explanation. They suggested that God actually pervades the Void with *hashgahah*, the divine 'providence' or 'oversight.' So it is not God, but God's providence that is still here with us, while God, the divine self, rules from a distance. They likened this to a king who oversees his domain from a castle—an ivory tower, if you will—where he remains unsullied by the day-to-day activities and affairs of his kingdom.[16]

This was the hold-out position of the theists. Before long, however, the pantheistic reality-map of Hasidism and its radical interpretation of *tzimtzum* proved too compelling for most to resist.

---

15 *Tikkunei Zohar*, Tikkun 57, 91b.
16 Gurary, *Chasidism*, 104.

# AQUARIUS —
## PANTHEISTIC TZIMTZUM

IT WAS A third generation Hasidic master, Rabbi Shneur
Zalman of Liadi (1745-1812), who was the most
effective spokesman for a metaphorical, pantheistic
interpretation of *tzimtzum*. Answering the literalists, Reb
Shneur Zalman argued that, if God *'had to'* withdraw
from any 'place,' it would suggest that God's power is
limited, and also that God changes or is changeable.
This is not only philosophically unacceptable, it is also
unacceptable according to the scriptural tradition, "I am
God; I have not changed" (Mal. 3:6).

Reb Shneur Zalman goes on to demonstrate the
various inconsistencies in the reasoning of the literalist
interpreters. First, he says, it is impossible to apply
literal concepts from the material world to God who
is immaterial and incorporeal.[17] Also, to distinguish
between God and God's *hashgahah*, or 'oversight,' is
to carry the simile of the king overseeing a kingdom
too far. That may apply in this world, but with God,
it is impossible to say God's knowledge is something
separate from God's essence, for divinity is truly "one
in all respects."[18]

---

17 Ibid., 106.
18 Ibid., 106, and also Maimonides, *The Guide of the Perplexed*, 119.

Of course, some literalists counter that it is also a limitation upon God's power to suggest that God *cannot* withdraw the divine essence from a space. But Reb Shneur Zalman does not deny that it is possible; he only says that it did not happen that way, as shown by the proof-text, "Do I not *fill* the heavens and earth?" (Jer. 23:24) And because there is an exegetical rule in Judaism that says no verse in Torah may be excluded from a literal interpretation, it is necessary to accept this verse as literal, forcing one to read the 'withdrawal' of God from the Void as metaphorical! Otherwise, the two ideas would contradict one another. Thus, "No place is devoid of God," and *tzimtzum* is actually a metaphor for the 'concealing' of God.[19]

In the kabbalistic literature, God is often discussed as *Ain Sof*, a designation that is meant to preserve God's transcendence. *Ain Sof* may be translated as 'infinite nothing,' or 'without limits,' and is a way of talking about God as the Absolute. In philosophy, the Absolute is not limited by any attributes or parts. It is beyond perceptions, transcendent of all our concepts. This is the axiom around which all kabbalistic ideas of God must conform; they must preserve God's transcendence.

As mentioned before, this is not simply an example of later philosophy being imposed on Jewish ideas, but a notion found in Torah itself—"For I am God, I have not changed." So, given the absolute nature of God, it is obvious that *tzimtzum* cannot be taken literally.

---

19 See Gurary, *Chasidism*, 107-10, for a more thorough presentation of this argument.

Nevertheless, we still have a little untangling to do, because the Holy Ari's description of *tzimtzum* actually uses two different terms that refer to God—*Ain Sof,* 'without limits,' and *Or Ain Sof,* 'light without limits.' In the Habad school of Hasidism, founded by Reb Shneur Zalman, the former is often called *Atzmut Ain Sof,* referring to the 'essence' of *Ain Sof,* or divinity itself; whereas *Or Ain Sof* refers to a penultimate category of divinity.

What does that mean? The Hebrew word, *or,* 'light,' is used in this context to call to mind the ability 'to see' and 'perceive'; whereas in darkness, all is obscured and hidden. But we have already established that *Atzmut Ain Sof* is imperceptible; so what we are really dealing with here is *Or Ain Sof,* the highest, although still limited, 'conceptualization' of *Atzmut Ain Sof,* a penultimate category for understanding what is beyond our understanding. It is, in fact, *the divine metaphor.*

In Rabbi Aryeh Kaplan's words, *Or Ain Sof* filling all existence "alludes to every possible concept of perfection being included within [God's] absolutely simple essence."[20] These concepts of perfection are completely homogenous, having no distinguishable separation that might imply limitation in the divine essence. However, this penultimate to *Atzmut Ain Sof,* by its very nature, must also partake of "the infinity" of *Ain Sof.*[21] As we have seen before, just as infinity cannot be made finite, neither can the *Or Ain Sof* allow for the existence of anything separate.

---

20 Aryeh Kaplan, ed. Abraham Sutton, *Innerspace: Introduction to Kabbalah, Meditation, and Prophecy,* 121.
21 Ibid., 121.

In the midst of the *Or Ain Sof*, a 'lack,' or the 'concept of lack,' is created by a withdrawal of the divine light away from a point in the 'center' of the light. Without this *tzimtzum* of the *Or Ain Sof*, nothing—*no separate thing*—could have existed.

This is a necessary prerequisite, so that what is created is not overwhelmed by the homogenous perfections of the *Or Ain Sof*. And yet, we are told that this light was also "brought into existence for the purpose of creating the world."[22] This refers to the *kav*, the 'ray of light,' that penetrates the empty space after the initial withdrawal of *tzimtzum*. So even after the concept of 'lack' was created, a controlled ray of light re-entered the spherical space to create creation and fill the conceptual Void.

The purpose of the Void, or 'negative light,' created by *tzimtzum* is to act as a barrier against the *Or Ain Sof*, again, so that creation is not overwhelmed. This is what is referred to in the *Zohar* as the "lamp of darkness," an energy source that radiates darkness.[23] It "blocks out everything that could possibly exist but does not" because the *kav* penetrated it afterword.[24] Thus, it is said that God wrapped in a 'garment,' *malbush*—the *Or Ain Sof*—and then hid in the darkness.[25]

However, it is worth noting that a garment both conceals *and* reveals. The *Or Ain Sof* is a barrier against the *Atzmut Ain Sof*, the essence of *Ain Sof*, protecting the 'hiddenness' of the essence, or rather, protecting *us* from the essence; and yet, if one throws a sheet over a piece

22 Ibid., 121.
23 *Zohar* 1:15a.
24 Kaplan, *Innerspace*, 121.
25 Ibid., 122.

of furniture, the object is in a sense, 'hidden,' but the form is still perceptible, suggesting the possibility of what is concealed beneath. Thus, *Atzmut Ain Sof* is both hidden and revealed by the *Or Ain Sof.* So *Or Ain Sof* itself would seem to be the first *tzimtzum*, or 'concealment,' of divinity, and the creation of the Void a second *tzimtzum!* The latter allows for creation, but still requires some of the divine light in the form of the *kav* to affect that creation. This is the basic paradox: the *Or Ain Sof* had to vacate a space, leaving it empty of its light, but also had to re-enter the space so that it would again be full of light! So truly, there is "no place empty" of God.

At this point, it will be easy to have forgotten how we got here, and why. Some may even be asking again— what is the purpose of a metaphor of divine lack?

Well, if you will remember, we began by trying to explain how infinity could become finite; and we have succeeded in this, though it may not be easy to see at first. For *tzimtzum* (in the pantheistic reality-map) teaches us that this 'space' that is void of God "is only 'dark' and 'vacated' with respect to us."[26] The "darkness" radiated by the "lamp of darkness" is only perceptible to us. It is just a cloud of ignorance. For God, it is still light, as though the *tzimtzum* had never occurred!

This is all to say that the 'withdrawal' was not necessary for God, but was done for our sake. It is the 'hiding of God' that allows us to perceive ourselves as separate, and thus also, allows us to build a convincing

---

26 Ibid., 123-24.

and difficult barrier to overcome on the road to discovering God. The greater the barrier, the greater the wholeness that can come from it being overcome. But, in actuality, there has never been any separation from God—God is here, now, in this very space—"No place is empty of God."

Thus, Reb Shneur Zalman teaches us that *tzimtzum* is actually a 'concealment' rather than a 'withdrawal,' and applies to the *Or Ain Sof* alone, and not to *Atzmut Ain Sof*, God's essence, even metaphorically. God's light was never removed from the Void, and there never was a Void. It was merely concealed from our point of view. We are radically ignorant of God's immanence right here and now, in this wonderful fiction we call, 'Life.'[27]

---

27 In his *Miftahay Hokhmat Ha'Emet*, Rabbi Shaul Baumann attempts to bridge the gap between the literalist interpretation of the Vilna Ga'on and the metaphorical interpretation of Shneur Zalman of Liadi by suggesting that the divinity that is *not* removed from the Void is that of *Malkhut sheba Malkhut sheba Ain Sof*. That is to say, what is left of God is the divine quality of receptivity, which is itself the Void. Thus, God is still present, though the fullness of God is removed, leaving only an openness to creation.

# PART III
# A Meditation on
# *Tzimtzum*

# Deism, Theism, Pantheism
## & the Problem of Evil

IN THE DEIST paradigm, Moses would seek God in the Tent of Meeting, between the wings of the cherubim. Can you imagine the incredible density of God-presence that 'divine contraction' would produce? When the human being meets the *All-ness of Being*, the experience has such a high focus that the numinosity is almost fatal. What room is there for human beings in such a holy atmosphere? Even when Moses met God in the burning bush, the *mysterium tremendum* hit him with such profound force, with such weight *(kavod-kaved)*, it seemed that if he were to take but one step closer, his existence would be entirely extinguished, obscured.

Then, when the holy Temple was built in King Solomon's time, the Holy of Holies was put in the temple structure. Again, there atop the Ark of Testimony were the two cherubim and God's overwhelming presence. And now, it is not Moses, but the high priest who enters the Holy of Holies. But the sense of danger is still there; for even the high priest is only allowed in the Holy of Holies once a year, on Yom Kippur.

You see, the average person could not bear to live in the space occupied by God's compressed presence; but neither could they live without God. Living in the presence seemed impossible for some, and for others, the rules for how to prepare for receiving the divine presence seemed too numerous. The whole thing was too overwhelming; people just could not handle it and shied away. It seemed to assault their fragile experience of reality.

When God poured over Mount Sinai with smoke and the sound of the *shofar*, the people "saw words," trembled, and begged Moses, saying, "If God talks to us any longer, we are not going to make it! Please, go and be the 'go-between' for us!"[28] In other words, "Moses, please *tzimtzum* the experience down for us. If we have to deal with it un-*tzimtzum*-ed, we will be overwhelmed by it!"

In deistic *tzimtzum*, the separation from God was necessary to keep us—*as impure beings*—from being extinguished by the purity of God's presence. So we needed Moses, and later the high priest, to mediate that flow of divine energy for us.

The literal interpretation of the Ari's *tzimtzum* runs into the same difficulty. How can purity and impurity, good and evil, exist together? The idea was that when God 'contracted' away from the Void, the 'good' also went away. And where God was not, there was evil.

That gives *tzimtzum* a very negative flavor, as it is associated with the absence of God.

In the theistic paradigm, characterized by polarities, people wanted to ask—can we reverse the *tzimtzum*? Their deepest wish was for the Messiah to come and save them from the *tzimtzum* and its evils. They wanted to merge with the Good, the light and the bliss, and

---

28 Paraphrasing Exodus 20:16.

get away from the *Sitra Ahra,* the 'Other Side.' But, in assigning the Other Side to the Unconscious, we enlarged and energized the 'shadow,' and it got a greater hold on us.

When the theistic paradigm began to shift, people began to ask—where was God during the Holocaust? Where was the justice of God then? Something just did not seem to add up any more. The more they talked about it, the greater tension they felt. This is when people began to talk about the 'death of God,' and the 'death of the name of God.'

Now, the 'life,' 'light,' and the 'name' of God are equivalent. The withdrawal of light and life, and the death of the name, mean that the 'old interface' has ceased to work, and the 'new interface' has not yet arrived. As Thomas Altizer put it, there is no more God 'up there,' or 'out there'—God has poured the divine self into the world completely. Thus, in *Night,* Elie Wiesel describes seeing a little boy hanging from the gallows, "lingering between life and death" in agony, and says . . .

Behind me, I heard the same man asking:

"For God's sake, where is God?"

And from within me, I heard a voice answer:

"Where is He? This is where—hanging here from this gallows."[29]

That is to say, *tzimtzum* had become so focused in that moment, on that child, that Wiesel could no longer say that God was 'up there' or 'out there.' *God was dead.* The theistic God was no longer viable. The *tzimtzum*

29 Elie Wiesel, *The Night Trilogy: Night, Dawn, The Accident,* 71-72.

that meant the 'absence of God' had overwhelmed the 'God of Justice' who is opposed to evil. That model just could not work any more.

God had become so immanent that the way to God was no longer through prayer directed 'upward,' or 'outward,' but into the very core of our being. The polarity of 'good and evil' would not cut it any more.

Alan Watts once asked, "Where is God?" and answered, "On the inside of the inside; behind the inside!" That is the God who can reconcile all opposites, 'good' and 'evil' together.

The *tzimtzum* of the new paradigm, of this pantheistic reality-map, is no longer associated with 'evil' and the 'absence of God,' but with 'ignorance' and the 'concealing of God.' In this paradigm, God withholds the indwelling spirit from self-awareness. *Tzimtzum* is an act of compassion. Since only God can exist where God is, there is no room for us to exist and know God. Therefore, God hid from us.

# SCALING-DOWN THE LIGHT
## & ITS IMPRISONMENT

IN THE TEACHINGS of the holy Maggid of Mezritch, *tzimtzum* is seen as a sort of *mattan Torah*, a 'bestowing of Torah,' in which God, as our parent, makes a *tzimtzum* in order to impart ideas that are beyond the capacity of the recipient to handle, as Krishna does for Arjuna in the *Bhagavad-Gita*.[30] We need it scaled-down for us in the way a parent takes difficult ideas and scales them down for a child's mind. In the same way, God scales-down infinite ideas for our finite minds.[31]

But this kind of *tzimtzum* contains an 'expansion' that can be coaxed out; it is not only a prison for light. Amplifying the teachings of the Maggid of Mezritch, Reb Shneur Zalman of Liadi tells us that parents cannot teach their children the complexity of what they know without bursting the child's mind. So parents tell their children parables, analogues that make a *tzimtzum* for the child. Later, this parable can be re-explored and expanded to reclaim more of the truth.

In order for us to know God, God must hold back some of the light. We need just enough to illuminate us, but not enough to burn us up; enough to stretch us, but

---

30 See *The Song of God: Bhagavad-Gita*, 91-92.
31 See Zalman Schachter-Shalomi and Netanel Miles-Yépez, *A Heart Afire: Stories and Teachings of the Early Hasidic Masters*, 197-98.

not enough to break us apart. We feel that we have to stretch more and more, and the urge to stretch is built into the radiation of that light. We cannot get enough light to be really satisfied. The more light we get, the more we realize—*I do not have it yet; I have got to stretch more!*

The reclamation of this light is part of the evolutionary expansion of consciousness. The Maggid of Mezritch put it this way: God made 'something out of nothing' *(yesh mi'ain)*, and it is our work to take that something and turn it back into nothing again! As we said earlier, God is spoken of in the *kabbalah* as *Ain*, or 'Nothing,' because God is not-a-thing, but transcends all limited things. We are created from *Ain*, or 'Nothing,' and have this 'Nothing' as our basis. Thus, the Maggid tells us, we can take the limited *ani*—the Hebrew word for 'I'—and turn it back into the *Ain*, the unlimited 'Nothing.' We take it back to its source, beyond the 'concealing' of *tzimtzum*. The Ba'al Shem Tov once said, "There is no deprivation for God's holy ones, for they get beyond *tzimtzum*."

Once, on a Shabbat in the early 1940s, I meditated until five in the afternoon, transfixed in front of a tree. In the depth of that meditation, I saw the tree breathing! I had been contemplating the mystery of the power of the miraculous and a Hasidic teaching that pointed to this paradox . . .

*If God were totally absent, no created thing could exist; if God were totally manifest and present, no created thing could exist either! So how can the creature exist? God is concealed from us! For if God was fully revealed, we would faint and cease to exist!*

What does it mean to 'faint' away? If the soul manifests too much, it blows out all our circuits. The higher one goes, the more one is overwhelmed by the light. In our tradition, we say, 'They went out beyond their vessels.' *Tzimtzum* is the focused flow of God-energy that keeps us alive, but which generally stays out of our immediate awareness.

However, this tightly focused compression of light, also gives one a sense of the light's imprisonment, a sense of it being locked-in. In our own experience, one of the greatest fears we have is that we may only exist in our own heads. The dread is of a radical solipsism— *Maybe I'm just imagining the whole thing!* When the fear gets really strong, we pick up the phone and call a friend to reassure ourselves, or go to the refrigerator to eat something. We need some kind of immediate grounding.

Imagine what it is like to be God, to truly be the only One around. On the one hand, there is a wonderful sense of sovereignty to it, and on the other, the loneliness is tremendous. It is like the two competing fears and desires of human beings: one is seen in Puritan Massachusetts, and the other in Quaker Pennsylvania.

In Puritan Massachusetts, long ago, solitary confinement was the worst conceivable punishment for a person. But in Quaker Pennsylvania, in days past, a day of solitariness was a day in which one could meditate and, as the Quakers would say, "Bethink thyself!"

There is something about *tzimtzum* that has to do with the densest reality we can know, a reality so dense that there is no place to move. It is almost oppressive. A person who is going to die feels that death is inescapable; death has become totally dense to them. Thus, the ultimate *tzimtzum* that our ego can experience is to die, and thinking of it, you feel this *tzimtzum* tightening in your stomach.

*Tzimtzum* can also be thought of as a black hole—matter contracted inwardly upon itself and becoming more and more dense. People used to ask—What is on the other side of a black hole? Where does one come out? I think this is what death is for us. The ego goes through its ultimate *tzimtzum*, and then comes out on the other side. This is the metaphor of the "eye of the needle."

What is an idol? It is an attempt to make the infinite finite. Why should people take a sculpture, abase themselves to it, worship and adore it, if not for the need to celebrate infinity in the most focused way in the finite? To deal with something so vast, we sometimes have to make it small! This is also what a lens does for us. In the center of an optical lens, the vastness before us is concentrated in a tiny point. Thus, we can use the lens to concentrate the sun's rays on a point to create heat and start a fire. Why is that? Because the lens is able to make a *tzimtzum*, to draw the rays together in a point. It is almost as if, at the center of the lens, existence stops and is reconstituted to cast its reflection in an inverted image. The Christian mystic, Meister Eckhart said, "The eye with which I see God is the same eye with which God sees me."[32] There is only one *tzimtzum*-point, as it were.

Think of the first cameras; they were really just dark boxes into which a tiny point of light was admitted. When you make a dark box like this, you are essentially

---

32 Claud Field (tr.), *Meister Eckhardt's Sermons*, Sermon IV.

'breaking of the vessels' was like the water breaking amid the birth pangs, announcing the coming of new life. It is the Messiah or *Mashiah* that delivers that life through the narrow place, from Egypt, if you will. For the Hebrew word, *mashiah*, literally means 'anointed with oil,' which for us is like the lubricant that brings us through the difficult birthing spaces.[36] This 'anointing' that smoothes the way is the function of the *Mashiah*, which I believe is *always* coming.[37] The *Mashiah* on the horizon is one for the expansion of human consciousness.

---

36 See Zalman M. Schachter-Shalomi, "The Tree of Life is Awakening," *Opening the Inner Gates*.

37 For instance, for America (and most of the rest of the world), the *Mashiah* for slavery has already come.

# TZIMTZUM AS A FUNCTION
# IN JEWISH RENEWAL

BECAUSE OF THE paradigm shift that has occurred in religion today, most of the world's spiritual traditions will no longer be able to do business as usual. All of us have to adapt. The hard and fast changes that have occurred in recent history, science, and society have made it necessary for us to alter our traditions. But this also requires a keen understanding of what is essential to them, and what is superfluous.

The conscious changes we make to our religions today cannot be made without sophistication. It is simply foolish to do so; for unless the deep structures and functions of a religion are understood and truly appreciated, a mere cutting away of the bulk is not going do the job. A "tradition which does not admit of both conservation and change will be dead and gone."[38]

Some have tried to do this in Judaism in recent history, and being rationalists, ended up cutting the heart out of Judaism. While others, favoring the heart over the head, have tried to remove reason and the intellect. Neither camp respected the holistic 'organicity' of the tradition in their process. There are others out there who would like to see a return to the 'yesteryear' of Judaism; but we cannot afford to deny how our situation has changed and evolved. And yet, neither can we deny that Judaism

---

38 R. Balasubramanian, *Primal Spirituality of the Vedas: Its Renewal and Renaissance*, 6.

has deep historical roots and a remarkably diverse *magisterium*.

The 20th-century Indian philosopher, Sarvepalli Radhakrishnan, sums up the situation perfectly when he writes . . .

> The only revolutions that endure are those that are rooted in the past. We can make our own history, but we cannot do so at will, in conditions of our own choosing. Culture is tradition and tradition is memory. The duration of this memory depends on the continuous appearance of creative personalities.[39]

Those "creative personalities" are the ones who will adapt the tradition to new circumstances, endowing it with a new meaning. This is the real challenge of *tzimtzum*. For it is only by taking over and re-interpreting elements of our own *magisterium* that our tradition will survive in this new atmosphere.

How can we make a Judaism for the future? We need to understand more of the function of what we do in Judaism, and be less concerned with the details of how we do it. We also need to find better uses for our current social units.

What is the function of *tzimtzum*? It has both a 'concealing' function and an 'essentializing' function. How many oranges would you have to eat in order to get the amount of vitamin C contained in one tablet of vitamin C? Probably many more than you

---

39 S. Radhakrishnan, *Religion and Society*, 113.

could eat in one sitting. That is a *tzimtzum*. It does away with the bulk and ephemeralizes the essence.

Imagine a fertilized ovum. In it is the *tzimtzum* of a human being. Likewise, an acorn is a *tzimtzum* of an oak tree. *Tzimtzum* contains the seed of growth, as well as the seed of further seeding. For Jews, the Passover *seder* is also a *tzimtzum*, an attempt to teach the seed-light of Judaism in just one night, in one incredibly dense transmission! We take the most abstract notions of freedom and divine providence and reduce them to sociemes we can repeat each year in a new setting.[40] Then we see how much is carried over to the next year and the next generation. If you look at why most Jews are Jews today, it is likely that you will find a Passover *seder* somewhere in their past that, even in the most anemic form, contained in itself much of the larger message of Judaism.

In the same way, if we would make Jewish Renewal more effective, we need to be able to make a *tzimtzum* of it. We have to become more and more effective in making transmissions of Jewish Renewal.

In the distant past, if you wanted to write a book, it would take a great deal of time and a lot of costly materials. Think of all the people that had to be involved in producing the materials and the content of a holy book in the past. There was a whole social pyramid of people involved in one way or another. It took a village! And these kinds of pyramids produced much inspiring and wonderful material. But it is not going to work in the same way for us.

---

40 In cultural anthropology, sociemes represent an 'action' that a special group does together. *Mitzvot* are sociemes in that sense.

We need to create smaller, less time-and-space-consuming systems and tools, while ever increasing our effectiveness. We need to be able to pack more information and God-consciousness into smaller ergs of expended energy.[41]

Yet each change we make in this direction must also be considered with an eye to its consequences. For instance, we can afford to have a Passover *seder* once a year, but we cannot afford to have one every week. It would not be Passover any more if we had it every week; part of its power comes from having it only once a year.

However, the functions of our everyday spiritual life have to be made more and more effective in order to work for us today. Every aspect of life—our use of time and energy—has to become more effective than it has been up to now. We have to take the 613 *mitzvot*, our inherited God-connections, and bring about a *tzimtzum* with them also. This is hard to say, but there are just too many details in them. But when we ask—how are we going to make a Judaism for the future? Then it is clear that we have to ephemeralize the container. And who is going to handle that? Are we going to wait for a new revelation from above?

One can almost hear a kind of laugh coming from the other side of *tzimtzum*. It seems to be saying—Hey, you know so much about the 'workings' now, the rest is up to you! After all, you're building your own atomic

---

41 In physics, an erg is a unit of work, or energy, in the metric system, being the work done by one dyne (unit of force) acting through the distance of one centimeter.

# Appendix A
## The Origin and Meaning
## of the Word, Tzimtzum

Every Hebrew word is derived from a three-letter root that gives us a clue as to the evolutionary development of all the words derived from that root. Most scholars believe that these Hebrew roots are tri-literal, or comprised of strings of three consonants. Nevertheless, there is also a bi-literal theory of two-consonant Hebrew roots developed by a French polymath, Fabre d'Olivet, in his book, *The Hebraic Tongue Restored*.

Writing in the 19th-century, d'Olivet believed that one could not possibly understand what the Bible had to say unless one also understood the original Hebrew. But in seeking out sources for his study of Hebrew, he found that the available Hebrew grammars of the day had merely attempted to squeeze the Hebrew language into a Latin or Greek framework. Thus, d'Olivet decided to begin his own investigation into what Hebrew had to say about *itself*. From this original study, he evolved his own unique theory of bi-literal Hebrew roots, asserting that Hebrew words do not originate in three-consonant roots, as is usually taught, but in two-consonant roots that are expandable to three.

Interestingly enough, the word *tzimtzum* repeats its two-consonant root, *Tzaddi-Mem*, and thus demonstrates a curious morphological tendency of the letter *Tzaddi*. It is a tendency to repeat itself sequentially when paired with another consonant, as we see in Hebrew words like *tzaltzel* and *tza'atzu'a*. The two-consonant root in the first half of the word carries the basic meaning, but the repeated sound in the second half of the word sets up the idea of 'process' and intensifies the basic meaning.

In his book, d'Olivet defines the root *Tzaddi-Mem* as meaning, "That which is carried with avidity, with force toward a thing; that which covets and seizes eagerly."[42] From this root meaning, we get a series of words in Hebrew like 'thirst,' 'fast,' and 'knot,' all of which strongly convey the idea of a tight focus. It gives one the feeling of something honing-in from the outside; you can almost feel the constricting energy in it.

Adding a third letter to *Tzaddi-Mem*, we discover then that all the words constructed have something to do with 'binding-together,' 'tightening-up,' or 'closing-down.' The word *tzamag, tz'mig*, a 'bottle-stopper,' becomes the word 'tire,' because air is blown-in and it is closed-up. And *tzamad, tzemed bakar* is when you take several cattle and tie them together under one yoke. So it is very much like the example given in the 13th-century text quoted earlier, as if someone had taken a deep inhalation and then quickly pursed their lips to hold it in.[43] Thus, d'Olivet's bi-literal theory gives us a unique insight into the possible origins and evolution of the word *tzimtzum*.

---

42 Fabre d'Olivet, tr. Nayán Louise Redfield, *The Hebraic Tongue Restored*, 435.
43 Gershom Scholem, *Kabbalah*, 129.

# Appendix B
## The Ari's *Tzimtzum*

Know this . . .
Before Emanations
And Creations,
A Simple Light
Filled all of
Existence.

All was Full
With Simplicity,
With Infinite Light.

No beginning,
No end;
All was One
Uniform Light.

Now, the Will
To create Worlds
And Emanations
Emerged.

Now, the Infinite
Contracted Self
In the Center
Of Its Light,

Withdrawing
From that Center
To the sides
Surrounding,
Leaving an
Empty Space,
A Void.

Contraction,
Completely uniform
Around a Center,
A Void,
Uniformly circular
On all sides.

Not shaped
Squarely
With corners fixed,
The Infinite
Contracted Self
As Circle,
Uniformly Round.

The Infinite Light
Absolutely same,
Wholly uniform,
Needing to contract
Uniformly,
Could not Contract Self
From one side
More than another.

The geometric science
Says there is no shape
Except the circle
The same all over;
Not the square,
With corners protruding,
Not the triangle,
Nor any other.

The Infinite,
Uniform in all things,
Needed to contract Self
As Circle:
Says the *Zohar*—
"It is a vessel
Round as the letter *Yud.*"
Says the *Zohar*—
"The Palaces
And what they contain
Are circles."

After the Contraction,
The Void vacant,
Empty Space
Remained in the Center
Of Infinite Light.

A Place was There
For What would Be
Emanated,
Created,
Formed,
Made.

Now,
One ray true,
Extending from
Infinite Light,
Extending from
A Circle of Light,
From Above to Below,
Descending,
Developing
Into the Void.

The top,
Extending from
Infinite Self,
Touches it;
The extemity,
The lower end,
Touches not
The Infinite Light.

The Infinite Light
Extends
Though the line
Spreading
Downward.

Within the Empty Place,
Emanating,
Creating,
Forming,
Making
All the Worlds,
Every one.

This ray,
A narrow channel,
Through which
Celestial Waters
Of Infinite Light
Pour and are drawn
Into the Worlds
In the Empty Space,
In the Void.

— Hayyim Vital, *Etz Hayyim*

# APPENDIX C
## THE ALTER REBBE'S *TZIMTZUM*

THE KABBALISTS SPEAK OF *Or Ain Sof*, the 'infinite light of divinity,' which is a lesser reflection of *Ain Sof*, the 'infinite nothing,' a reflection of its sovereignty.

It was within this infinite light of divinity that the *tzimtzum*, the 'contraction' mentioned in the *Etz Hayyim*, occurred. This contraction formed a *halal ha'panui*, a 'hollow space' or 'void' in the midst of the infinite light, in the infinite light of divinity, not in divinity itself, not in the infinite One, God forbid.

This *tzimtzum* was for the sake of bringing the physical world into existence, thus allowing human beings to bring about a revelation of God's infinite sovereignty in this world, just as it was before creation; for prior to creation, the infinite light of divinity filled all of existence, and this will ultimately be revealed again in the physical world, unrestrained by the contraction of light. Thus it is written, "I am first and I am the last, and there is no god but Me."

"I am first," refers to the state of existence prior to the *tzimtzum*. "Last," refers to the end of things, beyond creation, when "God alone will prevail." "There is no god but Me," refers to the time between, in the midst of the contraction, when we say, "we have no sovereign other than You," despite the concealment. This is the revelation that overcomes the concealment and hiding of the light.

This light comes through Torah, as it says, "The Torah is light," so that even now, in the midst of the *tzimtzum*, Torah channels and brings about a revealing of the infinite light of divinity, just as before the *tzimtzum*.

— Shneur Zalman of Liadi, *Torah Or*, MiKetz 39a.

# Appendix D
## Rebbe Nahman's *Tzimtzum*

### 1.

God, for mercy's sake,
Created the world
To reveal mercy;
For if there were no world,
On whom would mercy take pity?

So, to show God's mercy,
God created the Worlds—
From the peak of Nearness *(Atzilut)*
To the very center of the Earth!

Now God wished to create,
But there was not a where
In which to do it,
For all was Infinitely God *(Ain Sof),*
Blessed be that One-ness!

Therefore, God condensed
The Infinite Light *(Or Ain Sof)*
That filled all of existence
Sideways—and thus was space made,
An empty Void *(halal ha'panui).*

In that space,
'Days' and 'measures' came into being,
And thus the world was created.

This Void was needed
For the world's sake,
So that it could be put into a place.

Don't strain to understand the Void!
It is a Mystery not to be realized
Until the future is the now;
For about the Void,
We must say two opposing things:
It-Is and It-Is-Not.

The Void is the result
Of the contraction *(tzimtzum)*,
In which God withdrew
From that space
For the world's sake;
But the truth of the truth is . . .
God is still there.
For without God's
Life-giving energy,
Nothing could exist!

Thus, there is no way
To grasp the Void
Before the future is the now.

2.

You should know that
There are two kinds of unbelief:
One that originates with
The outer, external sciences . . .
The questions raised by them
Can be answered;
As it is written . . .
"Know what to answer
The unbeliever *(epikoros)*"
For outer knowing is still rooted
In the order of holiness.

For at the breaking
Of the vessels *(shevirat ha'kelim)*,
The holy light was so
Overwhelmingly powerful,
That it burst the vessels
That were meant to hold it!

And when these vessels burst,
The fragments of holiness took form,
Becoming the outer, external sciences.

So you see, even from holiness
There is a kind of dross, or slough;
Just as the body sweats and excretes
And must remove hair and nails,
So too, holiness has its slough;
These are the outer sciences
And the knowledge of externals.

When this slough is used
For the sake of power,
To twist the world,
You have source-ery,
Which has likewise fallen
From a higher wisdom.

One who can,
Should strive to avoid
The trap of the outer sciences;
But even if one should stumble
And fall into this trap,
All is not lost.

For one who seeks God,
Can surely find God,
Even there, amidst the shards
And sparks *(nitzotzot)* of holiness
That give life to these sciences,
Even in the very signs and symbols
By which these sciences express themselves!
For as long as there is rhyme and reason,
There is holiness in the form of the sparks;
As long as there is life in the world,
God is in the world too;
As long as the sparks are present,
Unbelief allows for a reply,
And for a return to holiness;
Thus, it is written . . .
"Know how to answer
The unbeliever *(epikoros)."*

But there is another kind of unbelief,
Rooted in un-wisdom,
Though it seems profound
For being un-real-izable,
Yet its 'profundity' is nonsense;
Such nonsense is often thought wise,
And one who is unlearned
Will often be stumped by it;
Being caught in a web of false reason,
How can one unmask it?
If one has no true knowledge,
One thinks the dissembler wise.

Likewise, the sophists
Make objections to true knowledge,
Issuing questions and answers
That are not rooted in wisdom,
But rather in un-wisdom.

Because human sense and reason
Knows not how to settle these issues,
The questions seem profound.

But in truth, there is no settling them,
For they come not from the sparks
Of holy somethingness,
But from the Void
Of unholy nothingness;
This is Void even of God,
So there is no way to find God there,
And no way to reply or repent.

If one could find God there,
There would be no Void,
Only Infinite God *(Ain Sof)*.

Therefore, there is no way
To answer this unbelief, as it is said,
"One who goes there cannot return."

How can the God-wrestler *(Yisra'el)*
Face the Void and live in it with God?

The God-wrestler believes
And skips over the sciences,
The lore of the Void,
Because with simple faith,
They know that God
"Fills and surrounds all worlds."

And the Void?
It is actually nothing,
And takes up no space at all;
All it does is separate
Between the divinity which "fills,"
And the divinity which "surrounds."

Without the Void,
All would have been One,
But then there would not
Have been any creature,
Or any world in existence;

So the Void is a kind of
Divine wisdom of not-being,
Allowing for separation between
One kind of being and another.

This wisdom of not-being,
The wisdom of the Void,
Cannot be realized!
It is not a something, and yet,
It makes all somethings possible;
Each something is infused with God
And surrounded by God,
But in-between is the Void that is not.

This simply cannot be known by knowing,
But it can be faithed by faithing
Through and beyond it.

This is why the God-wrestlers *(Yisra'el)*
Are called Hebrews *(Ivri'im),* 'through-passers,'
And why God is known as
"The God of the Hebrews,"
'The ones who have passed beyond.'

The wisdom of the Void is dangerous,
Because where it is strong,
There is no sense and no knowing.
So, be guarded and seek to escape
The snare and trap of the Void,
For "One who goes there cannot return."

3.

Know this . . .
There is one *tzaddik,*
A 'Moshe,' who must
Study the Void-thoughts,
Although there is
No settling these issues;
By entering the Void,
He raises the lost souls
Who have become
Entangled in the Void's web,
Souls that want to
Voice their objection
Amidst the mass of
The Void's unreason;
But no voice can
Carry in that emptiness,
Where there are no words;
For in the Void,
There is only silence.

All creation comes
From the word . . .
"By the word of God
Heaven was made,
By the breath of the mouth,
All their hosts"
For wisdom and sense
Inheres in the words.

All speech is bordered
By the five limits of the mouth;
Thus, all creation is limited
Within five dimensions . . .
"In wisdom have You
Made them all."


The Void has no limits,
No echo—burning questions
Are not answered there;
Those who have seen
The martyrs of Torah,
Want to know, "Why?"
And are answered with "Silence—
Thus is the decree of Thought!"
Such thought is not given to words,
Such thought is void of words.


But this *tzaddik* who is like Moshe
Is tongue-tied and used to thought
That cannot be worded,
And must give thought to the Void
In order to save the souls who are lost.


4.
How is the Void made?
By strife . . .
One *tzaddik* says this
And the other that,
And between there is
Strained a void;

Difference serves the purpose
Of making the Void . . . void.

Thus, there is space
For a whole world
To settle between them;
In this sense, the *tzaddikim*
Help the Creator to create;
Of this, *tzaddikim* must not
Talk over much;
Words are enlightening,
And too many words
Create too much light;
This causes a 'breaking,'
Leaving more shells and shards,
More evil and dross;
All talk must be limited to
The limit of the Worlds.

Thus it is said,
"All my days
I grew among the wise
And found nothing
Better than silence;
One who multiplies words
Multiplies sin and pollution."
The furies of the world
Are made from too much talk.

5.

A *tzaddik* is a singer,
And if the *tzaddik* is a 'Moshe,'
Souls lost in the Void
Can be lifted up
With that Moshe-song!

Every science
Has its own song;
Every science
Issues from a melody;
Even the un-wisdom of the Void
Has a melody of its own.

Thus, the Sages asked—
"What was wrong
With the heretic?"
They answered themselves—
"Greek songs never
Ceased from his lips;
All day he hummed
From the songbook
Of the Greeks."

You see, the song and the heresy
Each depend on the other—
The wisdom and its tune,
The science and its scale.

For heresies fall in book-loads
From the one who sings
The tune of heresy.

Every wisdom draws
From its own melody;
Even the higher ones
Draw from melodies higher up,
Up even to the point
Of the first emanation *(Atzilut),*
Beyond which there is nothing
But the Infinite Light *(Or Ain Sof)*
Surrounding the Void,
Which contains the something.

In the beyond of the Void,
There, too, is wisdom,
But it is Infinite Wisdom
And only the Infinite One *(Ain Sof)*
May attain to it;
God's wisdom cannot be
Reached at all:
There is nothing there,
Save faith—
To faith in God,
The blessed and holy One—
That God's Light embraces the All
Endlessly surrounding all worlds!

And faith, she is also a song
With a tune unique to her faithing.

Even those who worship
The stars and constellations,
Mistaking symbols for reality,
Have a special tune for each star,
For each sign of the Zodiac,
To which they sing and by which they
Celebrate in their houses of prayer.

Conversely, in the true
Worship of holiness,
Each faith has a special
Tune and song,
Attuned to the song
Of faith, most high,
The faith transcending
All wisdoms,
That faith in the
Self of the Endless Light *(Or Ain Sof)*,
Bathing all worlds in its radiance,
Which also has a song and a tune,
Beyond any other belonging
To other wisdoms and creeds;
Yet they all derive a note,
A phrase, a pattern and inspiration
From that tune, most high,
Which passes all understanding.

And when the future becomes the now,
All nations will have mouths of purity,
Calling with the Name *Y-H-V-H,*
All faithing in the One, fulfilling the words—
"Sing from the heart-springs of faith,"
The tune most sublime.

Now, only a *tzaddik* like Moshe
Merits to know this tune,
The song of silence—"Be still!"
Thus, the thought arose
That was beyond words and expression.

And this is why it is said,
"Then will Moshe sing,"
For that song has not yet been sung,
For it is a dead-raising song of silence.

And through this *tzaddik*'s *niggun*—
When that tongue-tied Moshe sings—
All the lost souls will rise from the abyss
To find their way out of the Void;
All tunes are re-absorbed
In the song of silence,
Where all heresies are
Integrated and dissolved,
Both tune and word,
In the great song of thought.

6.

And this is why God
Says to Moshe,
"Come to Pharaoh"—
The obstacle to freedom,
The Void-weaver—
"For I have made his heart
Heavy and hard."
For in the Void,
Only the hard questions,
And the contradictions remain . . .
Thus, Moshe comes to the Void
Where no one else may come,
For it is void of God, voided by God,
"So that I might set forth
My wonders in its midst."
The wondrous creation
Which needs a Void to hold it,
"In order that you may tell it
In the hearing of every
Child and grandchild."

For, in the creation,
In the some-thing,
You can tell and talk,
For there is a multiplicity
Of names and forms,
Letters and phrases,
Notes and songs,
All for mercy's sake.

For all mercy was condensed
So that the world could contain it:
Mercy is the world's possibility.

And the child and grandchild
Are mercy's special objects,
And can be told some-thing for pity's sake,
"That which I mocked-up in Egypt" —
For it is all a game, a monkey-shine, a circus
Made from the junk of broken vessels,
Still iridescent with the residue of holiness,
So that even there, in that place,
"You may know that I am God."

So that even in the middle of the joke,
In the middle of the shards,
In the middle of the heresy,
The partial and broken truth,
Even there you can know God,
The blessed and holy One!

"Know how to answer the unbeliever"
With that portion of truth most needed
To ply them and mend their partial truth.

"Moshe came to Pharaoh,"
The Void, and said, "Tomorrow
I bring the *Arbeh* (the swarms)
Of locusts into your midst."
For tomorrow is the time of receiving reward.

What is the reward all about?
To perceive great perception,
To have cosmic insight, today unattainable.


And then we will know
How the Void was like the locust,
Its cloak and being one,
All veils and garments;
But God outer, inner God,
Word and wordless God,
End and endless God,
Tune and singer God,
Most high and abyssal God,
Void God, Fullness God,
I-God, You-God, God-God!
Be-it-so — Amen.

— Nahman of Bratzlav, *Likkutei Maharan* I, 64.

# BIBLIOGRAPHY

Asch, Sholem. *Moses*. tr. Maurice Samuel. New York: G. P. Putnam's Sons, 1951.

Balasubramanian, R. *Primal Spirituality of the Vedas: Its Renewal and Renaissance*. Delhi: PHISPC, 1996.

d'Olivet, Fabre. *The Hebraic Tongue Restored and the True Meaning of the Hebrew Words Re-established and Proved by their Radical Analysis*. tr. Nayán Louise Redfield. New York: Samuel Weiser, 1976.

Field, Claud, tr. *Meister Eckhardt's Sermons*. 1909.

Gurary, Noson. *Chasidism: Its Development, Theology, and Practice*. Northvale, New Jersey: Jason Aronson Inc., 1997.

Guttmann, Julius. *Philosophies of Judaism: The History of Jewish Philosophy from Biblical Times to Franz Rosenzweig*. Tr. David W. Silverman. New York: Schocken Books, 1973.

Kaplan, Aryeh. *Innerspace: Introduction to Kabbalah, Meditation, and Prophecy*. ed. Abraham Sutton. Brooklyn, New York: Moznaim, 1990.

Maimonides, Moses. *The Guide of the Perplexed*. tr. Shlomo Pines. Chicago: University of Chicago Press, 1963.

Prabhavananda, and Christopher Isherwood, tr. *The Song of God: Bhagavad-Gita*. New York: Mentor, 1972.

Radhakrishnan, S. *Religion and Society*. London: George Allen & Unwin, 1969.

Schachter-Shalomi Zalman, and Netanel Miles-Yépez. *A Heart Afire: Stories and Teachings of the Early Hasidic Masters.* Philadelphia: Jewish Publication Society, 2009.

Schachter-Shalomi, Zalman M. "The Tree of Life is Awakening: Spiritual Transformation in Messianic Times." *Opening the Inner Gates: New Paths in Kabbalah and Psychology.* ed. Edward Hoffman. Boston: Shambhala, 1995.

Scholem, Gershom. *Kabbalah.* New York: Quadrangle/New York Times Book Co., 1974.

Twersky, Isadore, ed. *A Maimonides Reader.* West Orange, New Jersey: Behrman House, 1972.

Vital, Hayyim. *Likkutim Hadashim.* ed. by Daniel Touitou. Jerusalem: Mevakkeshei Ha'Shem, 1985.

Weschler, Lawrence. *Seeing is Forgetting the Name of the Thing One Sees: A Life of Contemporary Artist Robert Irwin.* Berkeley, California: University of California Press, 1982.

Wiesel, Elie. *The Night Trilogy: Night, Dawn, The Accident.* tr. Marion Wiesel. New York: Hill and Wang, 1985.

# Author Biographies

Netanel Miles-Yépez is an artist, philosopher, and scholar of comparative religion, and co-founder of the Sufi-Hasidic, Inayati-Maimuni Order, which fuses Sufi and Hasidic principles of spirituality.

Zalman Schachter-Shalomi was a rabbi and scholar of psychology of religion, the founder of the Jewish Renewal movement, and was widely considered one of the world's foremost authorities on Hasidism and Kabbalah.